Occam
Programming Manual

occam is a trade mark of the INMOS Group of Companies

**Prentice-Hall International
Series in Computer Science**

C. A. R. Hoare, Series Editor

Published

BACKHOUSE, R. C., *Syntax of Programming Languages: Theory and Practice*
de BAKKER, J. W., *Mathematical Theory of Program Correctness*
BJØRNER, D. and JONES, C., *Formal Specification and Software Development*
CLARK, K. L. and McCABE, F. G., *Micro-PROLOG: Programming in Logic*
DROMEY, R. G., *How to Solve it by Computer*
DUNCAN, F., *Microprocessor Programming and Software Development*
GOLDSCHLAGER, L. and LISTER, A., *Computer Science: A Modern Introduction*
HENDERSON, P., *Functional Programming: Application and Implementation*
INMOS, *Occam Programming Manual*
JACKSON, M. A., *System Development*
JONES, C. B., *Software Development: A Rigorous Approach*
MACCALLUM, I., *Pascal for the Apple*
REYNOLDS, J. C., *The Craft of Programming*
TENNENT, R. D., *Principles of Programming Languages*
WELSH, J. and ELDER, J., *Introduction to Pascal,* 2nd Edition
WELSH, J. and McKEAG, M., *Structured System Programming*

occam™
Programming Manual

INMOS Limited

Prentice/Hall International

Englewood Cliffs, New Jersey • London • New Delhi • Rio de Janeiro
Singapore • Sydney • Tokyo • Toronto • Wellington

© Copyright 1984 INMOS Limited

All rights reserved. No part of this publication may be reproduced, stored in a retrieval system, or transmitted, in any form or by any means, electronic, mechanical, photocopying, recording or otherwise, without prior permission of INMOS Limited.

0-13-629296-8

PRENTICE-HALL INTERNATIONAL, INC., *London*
PRENTICE-HALL OF AUSTRALIA PTY., LTD., *Sydney*
PRENTICE-HALL CANADA, INC., *Toronto*
PRENTICE-HALL OF INDIA PRIVATE LIMITED, *New Delhi*
PRENTICE-HALL OF JAPAN, INC., *Tokyo*
PRENTICE-HALL OF SOUTHEAST ASIA PTE., LTD., *Singapore*
PRENTICE-HALL, INC., *Englewood Cliffs, New Jersey*
WHITEHALL BOOKS LIMITED, *Wellington, New Zealand*

ISBN 0-13-629296-8

Printed in the United States of America

10 9 8 7 6 5 4 3 2

Occam

Occam is a new programming language. It is designed to support concurrent applications in which many parts of a system operate independently and interact. Occam is relevant to many present day applications particularly those involving microprocessors and real time. Occam will be essential for future applications involving the interaction of many thousands of computing components.

The novelty of occam is in its treatment of concurrency. Occam enables the programmer to express a program in terms of concurrent processes which communicate by sending messages through communication channels. This has two important consequences. Firstly, it gives the program a clear and simple structure as the individual processes operate largely independently. Secondly, it allows the program to exploit the performance of many computing components, as each concurrent process may be executed by an individual processor.

Occam can capture the hierarchical structure of a system by allowing an interconnected set of processes to be regarded from the outside as a single process. At any level of detail, the programmer is only concerned with a small and manageable set of processes.

The initial version of occam is intended to allow programmers and designers to experiment with the use of concurrency in programming and system design. To avoid obscuring the treatment of concurrency, it has been kept small and contains a minimum of additional features. It thus forms an excellent basis for teaching, whilst also possessing sufficient capability to be used for real applications.

This manual contains an introduction to the principles of the language, a tutorial introduction to its central features, and a programmer's reference manual, providing full details of the language, complete with examples.

Contents

1	Introduction		
2	Tutorial introduction to occam		
		2.1	Building blocks
		2.2	Sequential processes
		2.3	Repetitive processes
		2.4	Parallel processes
		2.5	Input and output revisited
		2.6	Naming processes
		2.7	Alternative processes
		2.8	Arrays of processes
		2.9	Conclusion
3	Programmer's reference manual		
		3.1	Purpose, use and organisation
		3.2	Syntactic notation
		3.3	Primitive processes
			3.3.1 Assignment processes (:=)
			3.3.2 Input processes (?)
			3.3.3 Output processes (!)
			3.3.4 Wait processes (WAIT)
			3.3.5 Skip processes (SKIP)
		3.4	Constructs
			3.4.1 Sequential processes (SEQ)
			3.4.2 Parallel processes (PAR)
			3.4.3 Alternative processes (ALT)
			3.4.4 Conditional processes (IF)
			3.4.5 Repetitive processes (WHILE)
			3.4.6 Replicators (FOR)
		3.5	Declarations
			3.5.1 Variable declarations (VAR)
			3.5.2 Channel declarations (CHAN)
			3.5.3 Vectors of variables
			3.5.4 Vectors of channels
			3.5.5 Constant definitions (DEF)
		3.6	Named processes and substitution

Contents

Continued

3.7	Expressions and constant expressions	
	3.7.1	Arithmetic operators
	3.7.2	Comparison operators
	3.7.3	Logical operators
	3.7.4	Boolean operators
	3.7.5	Shift operators
	3.7.6	Clock comparison operator (AFTER)
3.8	Elements	
	3.8.1	Elements
	3.8.2	Numbers
	3.8.3	Local clock (NOW)
	3.8.4	Character constants
	3.8.5	Vector constants (TABLE)
	3.8.6	Character strings
3.9	Lexical and character representations	
	3.9.1	Identifiers and reserved words
	3.9.2	Character set
3.10	Syntax	
	3.10.1	Program format
	3.10.2	Syntax summary
3.11	Vector operations	
	3.11.1	Slices
	3.11.2	Slice assignment
	3.11.3	Slice communication
3.12	Configuration	
	3.12.1	Prioritised alternative processes (PRI ALT)
	3.12.2	Single processor execution and priority (PRI PAR)
	3.12.3	Multi-processor execution (PLACED PAR)
	3.12.4	Physical resource allocation (ALLOCATE)

Index

Occam
Programming Manual

1 Introduction

1 Introduction

A process performs a sequence of actions, and terminates. Each action may be an assignment, an input or an output. An assignment changes the value of a variable, an input receives a value from a channel, and an output sends a value to a channel.

At any time between its start and termination, a process may be ready and waiting to communicate on one or more of its channels. Communication is synchronous. When both an input process and an output process are ready to communicate on the same channel, the value to be output is copied from the output process to the input process. The input and ouput processes then continue.

Each channel provides a one-way connection between two concurrent processes; one of the processes may output to the channel, and the other may input from it.

A process may be ready and waiting to input from any one of a number of channels. In this case, the input is taken from the first channel which is used for output by another process.

Occam may be used to program a network of computers. Each computer with local store executes a process with local variables, and each connection between two computers implements a channel between two processes.

Occam may be used to program an individual computer. The computer shares its time between the concurrent processes, and the channels are implemented by values in store. Indeed, a program designed for a network of connected computers may also be executed unchanged by a single computer.

Tutorial introduction to occam

This section introduces the main features of occam, and shows how to build simple occam programs. It assumes that the reader has had some experience of programming.

2.1 Building blocks

There are three primitive processes from which all other processes are constructed.

An input process. The ? symbol denotes input.

channel ? variable

An input process inputs a value from the channel into the variable.

An output process. The ! symbol denotes output.

channel ! expression

An ouput process outputs the value of the expression to the channel.

An assignment process. The := symbol denotes assignment.

variable := expression

An assignment process transfers the value of its expression to the named variable.

These three primitive processes can be combined sequentially or concurrently to create more complex processes, and thus they form the building blocks for programs.

2.2 Sequential processes

In many applications it is necessary to do a number of steps one after the other.

Assume that we require a process to input a single value via an input channel named **chan1**, then to output the square of the value via an output channel named **chan2**

chan1 → | x   x∗x | → chan2

This is a sequential process, as the output cannot take place before the input has finished.

This process will normally be part of a larger design. For the time being, we will assume that the channels used to connect this process to the rest of the system have already been declared.

We will need a local variable, say **x**, which is to hold the input value. In occam, a declaration immediately preceeds the process to which it applies, and so we first need to declare the variable **x**, which is done as follows

VAR x:

Every declaration in occam is introduced by a keyword (such as **VAR**), followed by an identifier, or a list of identifiers. The declaration is attached to a process and this is signified by the colon. Next we state that the process is sequential

VAR x:
SEQ

The word **SEQ** must line up underneath the word **VAR**.

The first event in the sequence will be the arrival of a value via the channel **chan1** to be stored in **x**. To indicate this we write

VAR x:
SEQ
  chan1 ? x

We indent the input process to indicate that it is a component of the sequential process.

2.2 Sequential processes
Continued

The next process has to output the value of x∗x via another channel named chan2

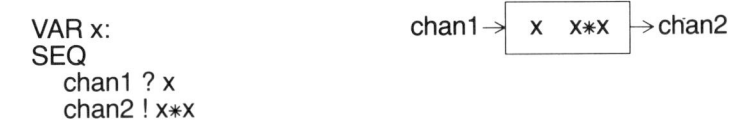

```
VAR x:
SEQ
   chan1 ? x
   chan2 ! x∗x
```

chan1 → [x   x∗x] → chan2

Note that the output process is again indented to indicate it is a component of the sequential process.

SEQ ensures that each component process terminates before the following component process is executed, and the entire process will only terminate when the final component process has finished. Thus once the output of x∗x has taken place, the sequential process itself has finished.

SEQ is an example of an occam 'constructor'. It builds a 'construct' (comprising the **SEQ** and its component processes), which, taken as a whole, can be regarded as a single process. Occam has a number of constructors, all of which are used in a similar way.

2.3 Repetitive processes

If we wish to square more than one value of **x**, we need to repeat the process that we have just written. To do this we use the repetitive process

WHILE x >= 0

This evaluates the expression accompanying it. If this expression is **TRUE** the component process will be executed. When the component process has finished, the expression will be evaluated again, and so on. As soon as the expression is **FALSE**, the repetitive construct terminates.

Thus for the example where we wish to square any number of successive values of **x**, we need the expression always to be **TRUE**. We can state this using

WHILE TRUE

Since the sequential process is now a component of the repetitive process, we must indent it

```
WHILE TRUE
    VAR x:
    SEQ
        chan1 ? x
        chan2 ! x*x
```

Because the **WHILE** expression is always **TRUE** the process never terminates. If we wish the process to square positive values of **x**, terminating when a negative value is input, we have to use the condition **x >= 0**.

To be able to do this, we have to arrange for **x** to be input before the **WHILE** is executed. This requires, therefore, another **SEQ** construct

```
SEQ
    chan1 ? x
    WHILE x >= 0
```

In the example above, **x** is declared within the repetitive process. Obviously **x** has to be valid for this particular sequence, so we have to move the declaration

```
VAR x:
SEQ
    chan1 ? x
    WHILE x >= 0
```

2.3 Repetitive processes
Continued

We have already input a value into x, so now all that is left to do is to output the value of x*x, and to input the next value ready to be tested next time.

```
VAR x:
SEQ
   chan1 ? x
   WHILE x >= 0
     SEQ
        chan2 ! x*x
        chan1 ? x
```

2.4　Parallel processes

If we require many processes to be running as a concurrent system, we can construct a parallel process. Here we shall take two processes which do not communicate with each other and run them in parallel, and then indicate a method by which parallel processes can communicate. A parallel process is not just limited to two components, of course.

Let us take the simple process described in section **2.3** which takes an input value from one channel, and outputs its square to another channel. The program is

```
WHILE TRUE
   VAR x:
   SEQ
     chan1 ? x
     chan2 ! x*x
```

We can take a similar process which inputs a value **y** via a channel named **chan3** and outputs y*y via a channel named **chan4**

```
WHILE TRUE
   VAR y:
   SEQ
     chan3 ? y
     chan4 ! y*y
```

We would like to execute these processes in parallel. We state this using the parallel constructor, remembering to indent the two component processes

```
PAR
   WHILE TRUE
      VAR x:
      SEQ
        chan1 ? x
        chan2 ! x*x
   WHILE TRUE
      VAR y:
      SEQ
        chan3 ? y
        chan4 ! y*y
```

2.4 Parallel processes
Continued

The parallel process causes the two component processes to execute simultaneously and terminates when its component processes have finished. The parallel process looks like

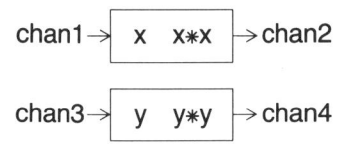

```
chan1 →[ x  x*x ]→ chan2

chan3 →[ y  y*y ]→ chan4
```

Notice that the order of the component processes in a parallel construct does not matter.

The above component processes do not communicate with each other. To illustrate how two concurrent processes can communicate with each other, we build a process which outputs x^4. This process looks like

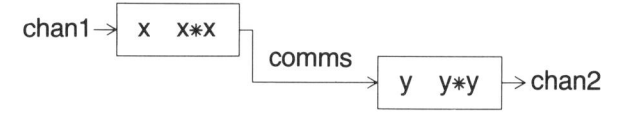

```
chan1 →[ x  x*x ]
                 ↘ comms
                         [ y  y*y ]→ chan2
```

For the parallel process we must first declare the linking channel, in this case named **comms**. This is done using

CHAN comms:

We next declare that the process is parallel and include its component processes properly indented

```
CHAN comms:
PAR
   WHILE TRUE
     VAR x:
     SEQ
        chan1 ? x
        comms ! x*x
   WHILE TRUE
     VAR y:
     SEQ
        comms ? y
        chan2 ! y*y
```

This completes the parallel process. If we require two-way communication between the concurrent processes we would need to use two channels. Notice that **x** and **y** are declared in the respective component processes.

2.5 Input and output revisited

Two concurrent processes communicate by using input and ouput. One executes an output to a channel, the other executes an input from the same channel. Input and output are synchronised. An input will not complete execution until an output on the same channel is executed, and equally an output will not complete execution until an input on the same channel is executed.

It is worth pausing to consider a little further what actually happens in the example given above. Both components of the parallel construct start executing in parallel. After a short time, the first one will reach its input process. A value is supplied via **chan1**, and the next thing that happens is that the first process reaches the output to the connecting channel **comms**.

Now consider the second process. There are two possibilities. Either the second process has not yet reached its input, in which case the first process waits until the second process does reach its input from **comms**, or the second process already has reached its input, and so is waiting for a value to arrive.

Eventually, the communication takes place, and both processes go on their separate ways. The output to **chan2** and next input from **chan1** can take place in parallel. The two processes will synchronise again to communicate the next intermediate result.

2.6 Naming processes

In the example of the parallel process above we had to write the text of both squaring processes. However, a name can be given to any process, allowing that process to be used by name when it is required.

If we are going to use a process several times, connected to the rest of the program in a different way each time, it is clear that the channels that are used on each occasion will be different. So let's rewrite the process, using non-commital names for the channels

```
WHILE TRUE
  VAR x:
  SEQ
    source ? x
    sink ! x*x
```

The process declaration allows us to give the process a name, for example, **square.** Parameters are added to indicate the non-commital names (often these are called 'formal parameters'). The process declaration is used in the following way to provide a squaring process

```
PROC square (CHAN source, sink) =
  WHILE TRUE
    VAR x:
    SEQ
      source ? x
      sink ! x*x:
```

Note that the squaring process itself is indented.

We can use this process simply as follows

```
CHAN comms:
PAR
  square (chan1, comms)
  square (comms, chan2)
```

2.6 Naming processes
Continued

Thus we can rewrite the entire program by combining this with the declaration of the squaring process

```
PROC square (CHAN source, sink) =
    WHILE TRUE
        VAR x:
        SEQ
            source ? x
            sink ! x*x:
CHAN comms:
PAR
    square (chan1, comms)
    square (comms, chan2)
```

Notice how in each use of the process **square** we specify which channels it is actually going to use (this specification is often called 'passing parameters'). For example, in the first use of the squaring process the channel named **source** now has the name **chan1**, and the channel named **sink** has the name **comms**.

2.7 Alternative processes

Sometimes a process has a number of channels associated with it and needs to perform one of a number of actions depending on which channel first sends it a message. This is achieved using the alternative process, which chooses just one of its inputs for execution.

As an example, a high-tech digital radio replaces an analog volume control with two buttons, one marked 'louder', the other marked 'softer'. These are connected to two channels, **louder** and **softer** respectively, and whenever either button is pressed it causes a message to be sent along the corresponding channel.

We need to design a volume controller process which will accept messages from these channels and transmit a message to the amplifier controller to indicate how loud the volume should be.

Let's look at the process which makes the volume increase. If the 'louder' button is pressed we wish the volume to increase, say by one unit. The volume is then transmitted to the amplifier. Name the channel to the amplifier **amplifier**. Thus the process is

SEQ
   volume := volume + 1
   amplifier ! volume

Similarly, if we want the volume to decrease by one unit then the corresponding process is

SEQ
   volume := volume − 1
   amplifier ! volume

When a button is pressed one of the channels is able to input. We are not interested here in communicating values along these channels, merely synchronising signals. The identifier **ANY** allows the values to be disregarded and a process to input if any signal is ready to be transmitted. The processes are inputs from the channels **louder** and **softer**

louder ? ANY
softer ? ANY

The controller needs to recognise which button has been pressed. We achieve this by combining these processes within an alternative process

ALT
   louder ? ANY
   softer ? ANY

2.7 Alternative processes
Continued

Note that the two component input processes are indented. We now need to add the processes which are to be executed if either of the alternative inputs is ready. These are again indented

```
VAR volume:
SEQ
   volume := 0
   WHILE TRUE
      ALT
         louder ? ANY
            SEQ
               volume := volume + 1
               amplifier ! volume
         softer ? ANY
            SEQ
               volume := volume − 1
               amplifier ! volume
```

This completes the volume controller process. The **WHILE TRUE** makes the process execute repeatedly for ever.

What if both buttons are pressed together? The alternative process guarantees that just one of its component processes will be chosen. If the buttons are pressed so close together that it is not possible to distinguish the times of pressing, one of the two processes will be chosen arbitrarily. The other one will be chosen on a later execution of the alternative process.

The inputs that are used for selection within an alternative process are called 'guards'. An input in a guard can be preceded with a condition, and then the guard is **TRUE** only if both the condition is **TRUE** and the input is possible

condition & chan1 ? x

Our simple example can be extended to include maximum and minimum volume. Thus if the radio is already at maximum volume and the louder button is pressed, we obviously do not want to increase the volume further. By using a guard expression, the process which increases the volume can be prevented from executing. The guard expressions are therefore.

volume < maximum   for louder
volume > minimum   for softer

2.7 Alternative processes
Continued

We can use **DEF** to give a constant value to the identifiers **maximum** and **minimum**

DEF maximum = 10, minimum = 2:

Thus a possible program would be

```
DEF maximum = 10, minimum = 2:
VAR volume:
SEQ
   volume := minimum
   WHILE TRUE
     ALT
       (volume < maximum) & louder ? ANY
         SEQ
           volume := volume + 1
           amplifier ! volume
       (volume > minimum) & softer ? ANY
         SEQ
           volume := volume − 1
           amplifier ! volume
```

2.8 Arrays of processes

We have shown how to build simple processes in occam, and now consider other methods of connecting processes. It is useful to be able to describe a collection of processes as an array of processes, which can be done in occam using a replicator.

A simple example is a process which takes a value and estimates its square root, using the Newton-Raphson approximation technique. The process needs the value (which we will call **x**) and an initial guess at the square root, for example half the value. A formula is applied to this initial guess to produce a better estimate. The same formula is reapplied to the new estimate to improve upon it. If the formula is applied enough times, the final estimate will be sufficiently close to the real square root. In this example, we will apply the formula a fixed number of times, and treat each application as a separate process, which we will call a Newton-Raphson step, **NRstep**.

We can consider this as a simple one dimensional array of processes with data flowing from the input to the output, sometimes called a pipeline. It looks like

```
x,x/2 ┌────────┐ x,est     x,est ┌────────┐ x,est    x,est ┌────────┐ root
─────→│ NRstep │──→  ..  ──────→│ NRstep │──→  ..  ──────→│ NRstep │─────→
      │   0    │                │   i    │                │  n−1   │
      └────────┘                └────────┘                └────────┘
```

Having established the overall structure, consider the individual process. Each step looks like

```
            ┌────────┐
values[i] ──→│ NRstep │──→ values[i+1]
            │   i    │
            └────────┘
```

The value of **x** and the value of the estimate from the previous step are input by **NRstep i** from channel **values[i]**. The values of **x** and the new estimate formed by **NRstep i** are output to the channel **values[i+1]**, which will be connected to the next process of the pipeline, **NRstep i+1**. The value of **x** is transmitted first, followed by the value of the estimate. To describe the process **NRstep i** in occam we first need to look at the Newton-Raphson approximation step. It provides the following formula for a new estimate, based on an existing estimate and the original value

(Estimate + (x/Estimate))/2

Each Newton-Raphson step **NRstep i** therefore outputs this value to the next step

values[i+1] ! (Estimate + (x/Estimate))/2

2.8 Arrays of processes
Continued

We now describe the process **NRstep i** in occam. We first need to declare the variables **x**, and **Estimate**

VAR x, Estimate:

The process needs to input **x** and the estimate from the previous step, and then to output **x** and a new estimate to the next step. It can be written in occam as

```
VAR x, Estimate:
SEQ
   values[i] ? x
   values[i] ? Estimate
   values[i+1] ! x
   values[i+1] ! (Estimate+(x/Estimate))/2
```

We can now use this process to construct the pipeline. The pipeline for the n-step Newton-Raphson approximation needs n+1 channels. Assuming that a constant **n** has been declared, we can declare the channels **values[0]** to **values[n]** using

CHAN values[n+1]:

We can form the pipeline consisting of **n** identical processes using **PAR** with a replicator. A replicator has the following form

i = [0 FOR n]

which means replicate **n** times starting from i=0, increasing **i** by 1. We can combine the channel declaration and the replicated **PAR**

```
CHAN values[n+1]:
PAR i = [0 FOR n]
   WHILE TRUE
      VAR x, Estimate:
      SEQ
         values[i] ? x
         values[i] ? Estimate
         values[i+1] ! x
         values[i+1] ! (Estimate+(x/Estimate))/2
```

We ensure repeated execution of each step of the pipeline with a **WHILE TRUE** construct.

2.8 Arrays of processes
Continued

Finally, we need two processes to connect this pipeline to the rest of the system. One inputs from the channel **Sq.root** a sequence of initial values, forms the first estimate and presents it to the pipeline:

```
WHILE TRUE
  VAR x:
  SEQ
    Sq.root ? x           -- input initial value
    values[0] ! x
    values[0] ! x/2       -- form initial estimate
```

The other outputs the final estimate to a channel called **Sq.root.result**:

```
WHILE TRUE
  VAR root:
  SEQ
    values[n] ? ANY
    values[n] ? root      -- receive final estimate
    Sq.root.result ! root
```

The entire process can be written as

```
CHAN values[n+1]:
PAR
  PAR i = [0 FOR n]
    WHILE TRUE
      VAR x, Estimate:
      SEQ
        values[i] ? x
        values[i] ? Estimate
        values[i+1] ! x
        values[i+1] ! (Estimate+(x/Estimate))/2
  WHILE TRUE
    VAR x:
    SEQ
      Sq.root ? x           -- input initial value
      values[0] ! x
      values[0] ! x/2       -- form initial estimate
  WHILE TRUE
    VAR root:
    SEQ
      values[n] ? ANY
      values[n] ? root      -- receive final estimate
      Sq.root.result ! root
```

2.8 Arrays of processes
Continued

In a conventional sequential programming language, the sequence of steps would be performed by a loop. For comparison, here is such a program

```
WHILE TRUE
  VAR x, Estimate:
  SEQ
    Sq.root ? x                -- input initial value
    Estimate := x/2            -- form initial estimate
    SEQ i = [0 FOR n]
      Estimate :=(Estimate+(x/Estimate))/2
    Sq.root.result ! Estimate
```

This inputs a value of **x**, and after the **n** steps of the loop have been performed, the final estimate of the square root is obtained. Another value for **x** is then input and the entire loop executed again.

By contrast, the pipeline inputs the next value for **x** and calculates the early estimates for its square root before the final estimate for the first value has been obtained. Let's look at the first two stages

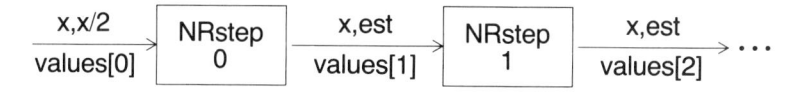

```
  x,x/2      ┌─────────┐   x,est    ┌─────────┐   x,est
─────────▶   │ NRstep  │ ─────────▶ │ NRstep  │ ─────────▶ ...
 values[0]   │    0    │  values[1] │    1    │  values[2]
             └─────────┘            └─────────┘
```

The processes operate in parallel. When the values of **x** and **x/2** are input on **values[0]** the process **NRstep 0** is executed.

When **NRstep 0** has output the new estimate via **values[1]**, **NRstep 1** is executed. However at this stage **NRstep 0** is ready to receive another value for **x**, and can be executed in parallel to **NRstep 1**. This does not affect the flow of the first value through the pipeline because it has already been output to **NRstep 1**.

Although the amount of calculation required for each individual result takes just as long with pipelining as it does with a conventional loop, the inherent parallelism permits the throughput of many values to be very much greater.

2.9 Conclusion

This section has introduced the main features of occam. The remainder of the manual gives full details of the whole language.

3.1 Purpose, use and organisation

This section provides the syntax and semantics of occam. It is intended primarily for reference, with each section on a separate page. Information is repeated where this can reduce the need for cross-reference.

The ordering of the sections is intended to provide a useful sequence to the knowledgeable programmer. The manual starts by defining the primitive processes and then details the different ways in which these primitive processes can be combined to create more elaborate processes. The next section describes declarations, and is followed by a section on the mechanisms for naming processes and substitution. This is followed by sections on expressions, elements, and the lexical and character representations. The final section provides a syntax summary.

Each section starts with a statement of purpose, together with small examples which are informally discussed. This is followed by the formal syntax of the language item and an informal explanation of its semantics.

3.2   Syntactic notation

The syntax of occam is described in a modified Backus-Naur Form printed in blue. Actual language symbols and keywords are printed in black.

The =symbol is used to define a syntactic category. The name of the category is given on the left of the symbol, and the valid syntactic forms on the right. Where there are several valid forms of one category, they are separated by the symbol |.

An item in curly brackets

{item}

indicates that it may be repeated zero or more times.

An item in square brackets

[item]

indicates that the item is optional.

As an example, the following are simplified definitions of operators and expressions

```
assoc.op    = + | *
operator    = + | − | * |/
element     = number | identifier | (expression)
expression  = element {assoc.op element}
            | element [operator element]
```

The following are therefore all legal expressions

```
2
x
x + y + z
(x − y) * z
```

Note that the rules for the format of occam programs are indicated informally in the syntax descriptions for each construct in the main part of the manual, but are not given in the syntax summary (section 3.10.2).

Alternative definitions for some syntactic categories are given in different sections of the manual, so that only the syntactic forms which are relevant to the construct being described are given in any one section.

3.3 Primitive processes

3.3.1 Assignment processes (:=)

An assignment process transfers the value of its expression to the named variable.

m := 1

assigns the value 1 to the variable **m**.

card[BYTE i] := ch

assigns the current value of **ch** to the **i**'th element of the vector **card**, addressed using byte subscription.

```
variable    = identifier [subscript]
assignment  = variable := expression
primitive   = assignment
```

The expression is evaluated, and the variable set to the resulting value. The assignment process then terminates.

The variable may be a simple variable, or an element of a vector of variables selected using either byte or word subscription.

See also

3.3.2	**Input processes**
3.3.3	**Output processes**
3.8.1	**Elements**

3.3.2 Input processes (?)

An input process transfers a value from a channel to a variable.

c1 ? x

inputs a value from the channel named **c1** to the variable **x**.

sync.chan ? ANY

inputs a value which is not preserved. It has the effect of synchronising the input with a concurrent process, which outputs a synchronising signal on the same channel.

link ? index; x

performs two inputs from the channel called **link**, placing first value in **index**, the second in **x**.

```
variable    = identifier [subscript]
channel     = identifier [subscript]
input       = channel ? variable {; variable}
input       = channel ? ANY
primitive   = input
```

An input sets the value of a variable to a value input from a channel. The input waits until an output using the same channel is executed in parallel with the input.

An input may also be used in a guard in an alternative construct.

A multiple input is equivalent to a sequence of separate input processes for each variable in turn, in left to right order. Each input is separately synchronised with an output process being executed in parallel. Each variable may be a simple variable, or a word or byte subscripted element of a vector of variables.

A channel may be a simple channel, or an element of a vector of channels.

If **ANY** is used instead of a variable, then the input value is discarded. This provides a mechanism for receiving synchronisation signals.

Only one of the components of a parallel construct may contain input processes for any given channel.

See also

3.3.3	**Output processes**
3.4.3	**Alternative processes**
3.4.2	**Parallel processes**

3.3.3 Output processes (!)

An output process transmits a value to a channel.

c[i] ! x

outputs the value of **x** to the channel indexed by the current value of **i** belonging to the vector of channels **c**.

letters ! alphabet[BYTE i]

outputs the i 'th byte of the vector **alphabet** to the channel **letters**.

sync.chan ! ANY

outputs an arbitrary value to the channel **sync.chan**. This would be used for synchronisation purposes.

```
channel    = identifier [ [ expression ] ]
output     = channel ! expression { ; expression}
output     = channel ! ANY
primitive  = output
```

The channel may be a simple channel, or an element of a vector of channels.

An output waits until an input using the same channel is executed. It then outputs the value of the expression to the channel and terminates.

A multiple output is equivalent to a sequence of outputs, and outputs the value of each expression in turn, in left to right order. Each output is separately synchronised with an input process executed in parallel.

ANY may be output in place of an expression, in which case an arbitrary value is output. This may be used as a synchronising signal.

Only one of the components of a parallel construct may contain output processes for any given channel.

See also

3.3.2	**Input processes**
3.4.2	**Parallel processes**
3.4.3	**Alternative processes**

3.3.4 Wait processes (WAIT)

WAIT is used to delay execution until a period of time has passed.

WAIT NOW AFTER alarm.time

continues execution when the time provided by the local clock is after the time stored in the variable **alarm.time**.

```
DEF timeout = 100 :
VAR clock, x :
SEQ
   clock := NOW
   ALT
      c1 ? x
         c2 ! ok.message; x
      WAIT NOW AFTER clock + timeout
         c2 ! timeout.message
```

waits until either a message is received on channel **c1**, in which case it is output to **c2**, preceded by a control value representing ok, or until the timeout occurs, in which case an appropriate control value is transmitted to **c2**.

wait   = WAITexpression
primitive = wait

A wait process is defined to be ready to execute if the expression evaluates to **TRUE**. The expression must be a clock comparison.

If a wait process is used as a primitive process, it delays until ready, and then terminates.

A wait process may also be used as a guard in an alternative process.

See also

3.4.3	**Alternative processes**
3.7.6	**Clock comparison operator**
3.8.3	**Local clock**

3.3.5 Skip processes (SKIP)

SKIP terminates with no effect.

```
IF
   (char>='0') AND (char<='9')
      SKIP
   TRUE
      char := 'x'
```

converts all characters which are not digits to character '**x**'.

primitive   =   SKIP

SKIP is always ready to execute, and its only effect is to terminate.

A skip process may be used as a guard in an alternative process.

See also

3.4.3   **Alternative processes**

3.4 Constructs

3.4.1 Sequential processes (SEQ)

A sequential process executes its component processes one after another.

```
VAR x:
SEQ
   c1 ? x
   c2 ! x*x
```

c1 → [x   x*x] → c2

inputs a single value from channel **c1** and then outputs the square of that value to the channel **c2**.

construct = SEQ
             {process}

A sequential process takes the form of the keyword **SEQ** followed by the component processes, each on a new line, all at an extra level of indentation.

The component processes are executed in turn. The sequential process terminates when the last component process has terminated.

If there are no component processes, the construct terminates.

See also

3.4.6   Replicators

3.4.2 Parallel processes (PAR)

A parallel process causes its component processes to be executed together.

```
CHAN comms:
PAR
   WHILE TRUE
     VAR x:
     SEQ
       c1 ? x
       comms ! x
   WHILE TRUE
     VAR x:
     SEQ
       comms ? x
       c2 ! x
```

c1 → [x] → comms → [x] → c2

The process constructed by **PAR** in this example combines two buffer processes which execute concurrently. Each of the buffer processes can hold a single value, so the effect of combining them is to repeatedly copy values from channel **c1** to channel **c2**, buffering up to two values at a time.

construct   = PAR
                 {process}

The keyword **PAR** is followed by a number of component processes, each starting on a new line and indented. The effect is to execute all of the component processes together, and the construct terminates when all the component processes have terminated. If there are no component processes, the construct terminates immediately.

Two component processes of a parallel construct may communicate by sending values using a channel. One contains outputs to the channel, and the other contains inputs from the channel. The two processes are said to be connected by the channel. No other component processes of the parallel construct may use the same channel. If two processes are connected by a channel, communication occurs when both the input and the output are ready, and the effect is to set the value of the variable specified by the input process to the value of the expression in the output process.

Variables are not used for communication between the component processes of a parallel construct. However, a variable may be used in two or more component processes, provided that no component process changes its value by input or assignment.

The rules governing the use of variables and channels cannot always be checked, particularly when using subscript operations.

See also   3.4.6   **Replicators**

3.4.3 Alternative processes (ALT)

An alternative process is used to accept the first message available from a number of channels.

```
WHILE TRUE
  VAR x :
  ALT
    c1 ? x
      c3 ! x
    c2 ? x
      c3 ! x
```

```
c1 ⟶
       ┌─────┐
       │  x  │ ⟶ c3
       └─────┘
c2 ⟶
```

This process merges data from channels **c1** and **c2** onto channel **c3**.

```
guard           = [expression & ] input
                | [expression & ] wait
                | [expression & ] SKIP

guarded.process = guard
                    process
                | ALT
                    {guarded.process}

construct       = ALT
                    {guarded.process}
```

An alternative process waits until at least one guarded process is ready to execute. One of the ready guarded processes is then selected and executed. The construct then terminates.

A guarded process starting with an input from a channel is ready if an output process is waiting to output to the channel. If the guarded process is selected, the input is performed, and then the component process is executed.

A guarded process starting with a wait is ready if the wait is ready. If the guarded process is selected, the component process is executed.

A guarded process starting with **SKIP** is always ready. If the guarded process is selected, the component process is executed.

If a guard contains an expression followed by an input or wait, the guarded process is ready only if both the value of the expression is **TRUE** and the input or wait is ready.

If a guard contains an expression followed by a skip, the guarded process is ready only if the value of the expression is **TRUE**.

3.4.3 Alternative processes (ALT)
Continued

If a guarded process is itself an alternative construct, then it is ready if one or more of the component guarded processes of the alternative is ready.

A guard containing a multiple input is ready if an output process using the same channel as the input is waiting. The guarded process is executed by performing all of the inputs of the multiple input in sequence, and then executing the component process.

If more than one guarded process is ready when the alternative process is executed, an arbitrary one is selected.

If more than one guarded process becomes ready at the same time, an arbitrary one is selected. This may occur if they contain inputs on the same channel.

See also

3.4.6   **Replicators**

3.4.4 Conditional processes (IF)

A conditional process executes the first component process for which the expression is TRUE.

```
IF
  i = 1
    out1 ! x
  i = 2
    out2 ! x
```

If the value of **i** is 1, then the value of **x** is output to the channel **out1**, if the value of **i** is 2 then **x** is output to **out2**. If **i** has any other value, the conditional process has no effect.

conditional = expression
             process
        | IF
          {conditional}

construct = IF
          {conditional}

A conditional taking the form of an expression followed by a process is able to execute if the expression evaluates to **TRUE**. A conditional taking the form of **IF** followed by component conditionals is able to execute if one of its component conditionals is able to execute.

The conditional process executes the first component (textually) which is able to execute, and then terminates. If there is no component able to execute, then the construct terminates with no other effect. At most one component is executed.

If there are no components, the construct terminates immediately.

See also

3.4.6   **Replicators**

3.4.5 Repetitive processes (WHILE)

A repetitive process executes the component process each time the expression evaluates to TRUE.

```
VAR x:
SEQ
  x := 0
  WHILE x >= 0
    SEQ
      c1 ? x
      c2 ! x
```

c1 → [x] → c2

This process provides a single buffer. It repeatedly copies values from the channel **c1** to the channel **c2**, buffering each value and terminating after copying a negative value.

construct = **WHILE** expression
                       process

The repetitive construct takes the form of the keyword **WHILE** followed by an expression, followed by a single component process indented on the next line.

The component process is executed repeatedly until the expression evaluates to **FALSE**, and the construct terminates. If the expression is initially **FALSE**, the process is not executed and the construct terminates immediately.

3.4.6 Replicators (FOR)

A replicator is used with a constructor to replicate the component process a number of times.

A replicator can be used with PAR to construct an array of concurrent processes.

```
CHAN c[n+1]:
PAR i = [0 FOR n]
   WHILE TRUE
      VAR x:
      SEQ
         c[i] ? x
         c[i+1] ! x
```

c[0] → ⎕ x ⎕ → c[1] ··· c[n−1] → ⎕ x ⎕ → c[n]

This process provides an **n** stage FIFO buffer. It repeatedly transfers values from channel **c[0]** to channel **c[n]**, buffering a maximum of **n** values.

A replicator can be used with ALT for inputting from an array of channels.

```
WHILE TRUE
   VAR x:
   ALT i = [1 FOR n]
      c[i] ? x
         c ! x
```

c[1] →
c[2] → ⎕ → c
c[n] →

This process merges data from a vector of channels **c[1]** through **c[n]** onto a single channel named **c**.

A replicator can be used with SEQ to provide a conventional loop.

```
DEF alphabet = "abcdefghijklmnopqrstuvwxyz":
SEQ i = [1 FOR alphabet[BYTE 0]]
   letters ! alphabet[BYTE i]
```

⎕ → letters

This process outputs the alphabetic characters in alphabetical order via the channel named **letters**.

3.4.6 Replicators (FOR)
Continued

```
replicator        = identifier = [base FOR count]
base              = expression
count             = expression
construct         = SEQ replicator
                        process
construct         = PAR replicator
                        process
construct         = ALT replicator
                        guarded.process
construct         = IF  replicator
                        conditional
guarded.process   = ALT replicator
                        guarded.process
conditional       = IF  replicator
                        conditional
```

The replicator declares an identifier to be the replicator index, giving its base value and a count of the number of replications required.

Its effect is to form a sequential, parallel, alternative, or conditional construct containing count components by replicating the component process, substituting successive integer values for the replicator index (starting at base). The substituted value for the replicator index in the last component will be (base + count) − 1.

The replicator index can be used in expressions (but not constant expressions) in the component process. It may not be changed by assignment or input.

An implementation may restrict the values of base and count to be constants, particularly when a replicator is used to form a parallel construct.

If count evaluates to less than zero or equal to zero, then an empty construct is generated. This has the effect of termination for sequential, parallel and conditional processes, and the effect of never being ready to execute for alternative processes.

Where textual order is significant, the component with the value base substituted for the replicator index is considered to be textually first, followed by the component with (base + 1), etc.

See also

3.4.1	**Sequential processes**
3.4.2	**Parallel processes**
3.4.3	**Alternative processes**
3.4.4	**Conditional processes**

3.5 Declarations

A declaration in occam is used to introduce an identifier.

A declaration introduces a new identifier for use in the process that follows it. It defines the meaning that the identifier will have within the process. If the new identifier is the same as an identifier which is already in use, all occurrences of the identifier in the following process refer to the meaning associated with the new declaration.

    process   = declaration:
                 process

Declarations introduced by **VAR, CHAN, DEF** and **PROC** are linked to the following process by a colon (:) at the end of the last line of the declaration. The process follows on the next line, at the same level of indentation as the keyword of the declaration.

An identifier may be declared as a formal parameter of a named process, and is used with the given meaning in the named process.

An identifier may be declared as a replicator index. It can be used in expressions (but not constant expressions) in the component process. It cannot be changed by assignment or input.

Depending on the implementation, variables, channels and vectors may require locations in store to be allocated. Such locations are allocated before the process following the declaration is executed, and deallocated when it terminates.

See also

3.4.6	Replicators
3.6	Named processes and substitution

3.5.1 Variable declarations (VAR)

A variable declaration introduces an identifier to be used as a variable.

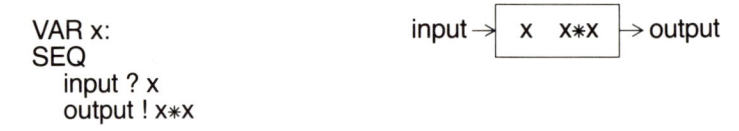

```
VAR x:
SEQ
   input ? x
   output ! x*x
```

input → | x   x*x | → output

In this example, **VAR x:** introduces the identifier **x**, which is used to hold a value within the **SEQ** process. Note that the variable named **x** cannot be accessed outside of this process.

```
var          = identifier
declaration  = VAR var {, var}
process      = declaration:
               process
```

A variable declaration introduces an identifier for use as a variable. The variable is not initialised, and therefore its value is not determined at the start of execution of the following process; it may well be different each time the following process is executed.

A list of variable identifiers may be declared. This is the same as a series of single variable declarations.

See also

3.3.1	**Assignment processes**
3.5.3	**Vectors of variables**
3.8.1	**Elements**

3.5.2 Channel declarations (CHAN)

A channel declaration introduces a new identifier to be used as a channel. Channels are used to communicate between concurrent processes.

```
CHAN c:
PAR
   buffer (c1, c)
   buffer (c, c2)
```

c1 → [x] → c → [x] → c2

In this example, the channel **c** is declared as an internal channel of the **PAR** process. It cannot be used outside this process. Note that channels **c1** and **c2** will be external to this process, and will be declared in an outer level declaration.

```
chan        = identifier
declaration = CHAN chan { ,chan }
process     = declaration :
              process
```

A channel declaration introduces an identifier for use as a channel.

A list of channel identifiers may be declared. This is the same as a series of single channel declarations.

See also

3.5.4   **Vectors of channels**

3.5.3 Vectors of variables

A variable vector declaration introduces an identifier to be used as a vector of variables.

VAR list [16]:

declares a vector of 16 variables. They are indexed as list[0] ... list[15].

VAR line [BYTE 80]:

allocates a vector named line with enough variables to hold 80 bytes.

```
subscript    = [[BYTE] count]
count        = expression
var          = identifier subscript
declaration  = VAR var { , var }
process      = declaration :
               process
```

A variable vector is a set of variables. The value of count, which must be a constant expression, gives the number of variables in the vector. The variables are numbered from 0 up to (count − 1). If count is preceded by BYTE, the value of count gives the number of bytes in the vector; the vector contains enough variables to hold all the bytes.

The identifier introduced by a variable vector declaration, may be used as an actual parameter to pass the vector to a substitution, or may be subscripted to access an individual variable in the vector. Subscription is described fully under Elements (section 3.8.1).

A list of variable vector identifiers may be declared. This is the same as a series of single variable vector declarations. Each vector is individually sized.

See also

3.5.1	Variable declarations
3.6	Named processes and substitution
3.7	Expressions and constant expressions
3.8.1	Elements

3.5.4 Vectors of channels

A channel vector declaration introduces a new identifier to be used as a vector of channels. Channels are used to communicate between concurrent processes.

```
CHAN c[n - 1]:
PAR
   buffer (c1, c[0])
   PAR i = [0 FOR n - 2]
      buffer (c[i], c[i + 1])
   buffer (c[n - 2], c2)
```

c1 → x → c[0] ··· c[n − 2] → x → c2

This example declares a vector of channels to provide the internal structure of a FIFO buffer of depth n. The value of n (a constant expression) and the channels c1 and c2 will be external to this process, and will be declared in outer level declarations.

```
chan         = identifier [count]
declaration  = CHAN chan { , chan}
process      = declaration :
                 process
```

A channel vector is a set of channels. The value of count, which must be a constant expression, gives the number of channels in the vector. The channels are numbered from 0 up to (count − 1).

A channel vector declaration introduces an identifier for use as a vector of channels. The identifier may be used as an actual parameter to pass the vector to a substitution, or may be subscripted to access an individual channel in the vector.

A list of channel vector identifiers may be declared. This is the same as a series of single channel vector declarations. Each vector is individually sized.

See also

3.5.2	Channel declarations
3.6	Named processes and substitution
3.7	Expressions and constant expressions

3.5.5 Constant definitions (DEF)

DEF associates a name with a constant value, or with a table of constant values.

DEF close.purge = 1, close.keep = 2:

This example associates the constant values with the identifiers **close.purge** and **close.keep**. Use of these identifiers within the subsequent process will yield the associated values.

```
DEF crctable =   TABLE [ #0000,  #CC01,  #D801,  #1400,
                         #F001,  #3C00,  #2800,  #E401,
                         #A001,  #6C00,  #7800,  #B401,
                         #5000,  #9C01,  #8801,  #4400
                       ]:
```

This example provides a definition of an identifier to represent a vector constant. Individual values may be obtained by subscripting the identifier **crctable**.

DEF alphabet = "abcdefghijklmnopqrstuvwxyz":

This example defines the vector constant **alphabet** to be associated with a string. Individual letters of the alphabet may be obtained by using byte subscription.

```
const.def      =  identifier = expression
                | identifier = vector.constant
declaration    =  DEF const.def { , const.def}
```

DEF declares an identifier, and defines it to be associated with a constant value. Each occurrence of the identifier in the subsequent process is replaced by the constant value.

Constants come in two classes: simple constants and vector constants. Both are introduced by the constant declaration.

Simple constants are defined by a constant expression (one which only involves operators, numbers, character constants, **TRUE**, **FALSE** and simple constants). A simple constant evaluates to a single value.

A vector constant associates an identifier with a table or string. It may be subscripted to produce a single value, or passed as a value vector parameter in a substitution.

See also
3.7	**Expressions and constant expressions**
3.8.1	**Elements**
3.8.5	**Vector constants**
3.8.6	**Character strings**

3.6 Named processes and substitution

A name can be given to the text of a process. The text will be substituted for all occurrences of the name in the subsequent process. Channels, variables etc. may be used as parameters when textual substitution takes place.

```
PROC buffer (CHAN in, out) =
    WHILE TRUE
      VAR x:
      SEQ
        in ? x
        out ! x:
CHAN c:
PAR
  buffer (c1, c)
  buffer (c, c2)
```

in → [x] → out

c1 → [x] → c → [x] → c2

A single buffer process is declared. The text for this is then substituted in the two components of a parallel construct to give a process which copies from channel **c1** to channel **c2**, buffering up to two values at a time.

The line starting **PROC** gives the name **buffer** to the process, and identifies two formal parameters, the channels **in** and **out**. The remaining lines give the text of the named process. This is written in terms of the local variable **x**, and the formal parameters **in** and **out**. The formal parameters will be substituted by the actual parameters when the named process is substituted in the subsequent process.

form.parm	= **VAR** identifier [[ ]] {, identifier [[ ]] }
	| **CHAN** identifier [[ ]] {, identifier [[ ]] }
	| **VALUE** identifier [[ ]] {, identifier [[ ]] }
form.parms	= (form.parm {, form.parm})
declaration	= **PROC** identifier [form.parms] =
	process
process	= declaration:
	process
process	= identifier [(expression {, expression})]

The **PROC** declaration introduces an identifier to name the process which follows, indented, on the succeeding lines. This process is referred to as the named process. This, in turn, is followed by the process in which the identifier will be used (the prefixed process). The named process will be substituted for all occurrences of the identifier in the prefixed process.

3.6   Named processes and substitution
Continued

The named process may have parameters. The parameters that are declared with the declaration of the named process are called formal parameters. Those supplied as part of the substitution are called actual parameters.

The following are the formal parameter specifiers

VAR identifier	variable
CHAN identifier	channel
VALUE identifier	value
VAR identifier[ ]	vector of variables
CHAN identifier[ ]	vector of channels
VALUE identifier[ ]	vector of values

The size of the vector is not specified in the formal parameter. Different sized vectors may be used as actual parameters on different substitutions.
The identifier of the formal parameter may be written within the text of the named process wherever a corresponding variable, channel, vector or value would be valid. A value vector parameter may be used as a constant vector in the named process. Value parameters and value vector parameters may not be changed by assignment or input.

The keyword **VAR**, **CHAN** or **VALUE** need not be repeated in successive items in the parameter list.

A substitution with parameters consists of the identifier of the named process followed by the actual parameters in brackets. A substitution without parameters consists of the identifier of the named process.

The effect of a substitution is to make a copy of the process named by the identifier, and to execute it in place of the substitution.

If the named process has formal parameters, then they are replaced by the actual parameters of the substitution, before the named process is executed. The actual parameters must correspond to formal parameters as follows

Formal	Actual
variable	variable or element of vector of variables
channel	channel or element of vector of channels
value	value of an expression
vector of variables	vector of variables
vector of channels	vector of channels
vector of values	vector of variables or vector constant

3.6 Named processes and substitution
Continued

All value parameters are evaluated, and all elements of vectors are selected before the actual parameters are substituted.

No recursion is allowed.

The named process may contain an identifier which is the same as an identifer substituted as an actual parameter. In this case, the actual parameter refers to the identifier in use at the point in the program where the substitution takes place.

An identifier which is used in, but not declared in, a named process is called a free identifier of the named process. A free identifier may be the same as an identifier in use at the point in the program where the substitution takes place. In this case, the free identifier is the identifier in use at the point in the program where the named process is declared.

A formal variable parameter cannot be substituted by a vector element accessed using byte indexing.

3.7 Expressions and constant expressions

An expression is evaluated to produce a single value.

expression = monadic.op element

An expression can take the form of an element preceded by one of the two monadic operators − or **NOT**.

expression = element [operator element]

An expression can take the form of a single element, or two elements separated by an operator.

expression = element {assoc.op element}

An expression may take the form of a sequence of operands separated by the same associative operator. The associative operators are

+	addition
*	multiplication
/\	bitwise and
\/	bitwise or
><	bitwise exclusive or
AND	Boolean and
OR	Boolean or

A constant expression is one which only involves operators, numbers, character constants, **TRUE**, **FALSE** and identifiers defined as simple constants. A constant expression may not involve variables or replicator indices. A constant expression evaluates to a single value and can be computed by a compiler.

3.7.1 Arithmetic operators

Arithmetic operators provide two's complement integer arithmetic.

addition	+
subtraction	−
multiplication	∗
division	/
remainder	\

The arithmetic operators treat their operands as two's complement integers. An arithmetic operator combines two single word values to produce a single word result.

Minus may be used with only one operand, and is evaluated by subtracting the operand from zero. The effect of minus applied to the the most negative integer is implementation dependent.

Division rounds towards zero, the sign of the result being positive if both dividend (left hand operand) and divisor (right hand operand) have the same sign, and negative if they are of opposite sign.

The remainder operator evaluates to the remainder when the left hand operand is divided by the right hand operand. The sign of remainder is the same as the sign of the dividend. The remainder is such that

$x = ((y * (x/y)) + (x \backslash y))$

is always **TRUE**, regardless of the sign of **x** and **y**.

The effect of division and remainder by zero is implementation dependent, as is the division of the most negative integer by −1.

3.7.2 Comparison operators

less than	<
greater than	>
less than or equal to	<=
greater than or equal to	>=
equal to	=
not equal to	<>

The result of a comparison operator is a truth value, **TRUE** or **FALSE**. The equal and not equal operators compare corresponding bits of their operands. The other comparison operators treat their operands as two's complement integers.

3.7.3 Logical operators

Logical operators provide facilities for bit manipulation and truth value manipulation.

i := crc /\ #F

produces a value in the variable **i** of between 0 and 15, by masking the variable **crc** with the hexadecimal constant #F.

The logical operators are

and	/\
or	\/
exclusive or	><
not	**NOT**

The logical operators operate on corresponding bits of their operands, producing bits of the result according to the following table

first operand	second operand	and	or	exclusive or
0	0	0	0	0
0	1	0	1	1
1	0	0	1	1
1	1	1	1	0

The logical operator **NOT** takes one operand. It is evaluated by inverting each bit of its operand.

3.7.4 Boolean operators

Boolean operators provide left to right evaluation of conditions. Evaluation ceases as soon as the result can be determined.

IF (i >= 0) AND (i <= tab.size) AND (tab[i] = 0)

In this example, checks are made on the value of **i** before it is used as an index for the table **tab**. This will ensure that no attempt will be made to use **i** as the index if it is out of range.

The boolean operators are

AND
OR

The result of evaluating an operand of a boolean operator should be either **TRUE** or **FALSE**. The result of the **AND** operator is **FALSE** if its first operand is **FALSE**, otherwise the result is the same as the second operand. The result of the **OR** operator is **TRUE** if its first operand is **TRUE**, otherwise the result is the same as the second operand.

3.7.5 Shift operators

The shift operators are

up shift   <<
down shift   >>

The result of a shift operator is its first operand shifted by the number of bit positions given by its second operand. The up shift operator shifts towards the most significant end of the word, the down shift operator towards the least significant end. In both cases, vacated bits are filled with zero.

Shifting by more than the word length results in zero. It is an error to attempt to shift by a negative number of places. Note that this will only be detected if the second operand is a constant.

3.7.6 Clock comparison operator (AFTER)

AFTER is used for comparing two time values derived from a cyclic clock.

```
DEF interval = 60:
VAR alarm.clock:
SEQ
   alarm.clock := NOW + interval
   WHILE TRUE
      SEQ
         WAIT NOW AFTER alarm.clock
         ring ! alarm.clock
         alarm.clock := alarm.clock + interval
```

causes the time to be output to the channel **ring** every 60 units of time. Note that it has been constructed to avoid any slippage of time resulting from the time taken to execute the **WHILE** process.

expression   =   element1 **AFTER** element2

The value of the expression is **TRUE** if (element1 − element2) > 0. It is used in **WAIT** processes to compare the value of element2 with the value of a free running clock, accessed as element1. Note that **AFTER** gives the desired result irrespective of the sign of element1 and element2. Note also that the maximum interval of time for which **AFTER** can be used is the interval which can be represented as a positive integer in a single word. Half the full cycle of values is regarded as 'after', and the other half as 'before'.

See also

3.3.4	**Wait processes**
3.8.3	**Local clock**

3.8	**Elements**
3.8.1	**Elements**

An element is used to provide a value in an expression.

The following examples of elements yield the values indicated

x	the value of the variable **x**
v[BYTE i]	the value of the **i** 'th byte of vector **v**
TRUE	the value represented by all 1's
'a'	the ASCII code of the character **a**
(x / y)	the value produced by dividing **x** by **y**

variable	=	identifier [subscript]
vector.constant	=	table l string
item	=	variable l vector.constant subscript
element	=	number l item l **TRUE** l **FALSE** l **NOW**
		l char.const l (expression)

An element produces a word value, represented as a pattern of bits. A word can hold an implementation dependent number of 8-bit bytes.

The value of the element **TRUE** is the bit pattern consisting entirely of one bits.
The value of the element **FALSE** is the bit pattern consisting entirely of zero bits.

The value of a parenthesised expression is the value of the expression. Parentheses are used to indicate precedence.

The value of an element which is a variable is the current value of the variable.

The value of an element which is a replicator index is the value of the base expression given in the replicator constructor, plus the number of the replication (counting from zero).

3.8.1 Elements
Continued

The value of an element which is a vector, followed by a subscript in square brackets, is obtained by evaluating the expression forming the subscript, and then using it to index the vector to obtain a value. If **s** is the value of the subscript, then the **s**'th word (counting from zero) is accessed to produce a word value, unless the expression is immediately preceded by the keyword **BYTE**, in which case the **s**'th byte is accessed, producing a value which is non-zero in the least significant byte only. The effect of a value for **s** which does not define a word or byte within the vector is implementation dependent. Byte zero is the least significant byte of word zero of the vector.

The value of an element which is a constant is the bit pattern representing that constant.

It is not permitted to use an identifier declared as a channel or vector of channels as an element in an expression.

See also

3.8.2	**Numbers**
3.8.3	**Local clock**
3.8.4	**Character constants**
3.8.5	**Vector constants**

3.8.2　Numbers

```
0
941
#FF
```
            the hexadecimal constant which is all ones for the least significant 8 bits

A number is written as a sequence of decimal digits and represents the corresponding value radix ten. Numbers are stored using two's complement. The number range which may be stored is implementation dependent.

A number may be written as the symbol # followed by hexadecimal digits, and represents the corresponding value radix sixteen (right justified). Either upper or lower case hexadecimal digits may be used.

3.8.3 Local clock (NOW)

NOW provides the value of the local clock.

alarm.clock := NOW + interval

assigns to alarm.clock a value which represents a short time after the assignment is executed.

element   = NOW

NOW is a word-sized integer representing the time. At regular, but implementation dependent, intervals of time it is incremented.

No relationship may be assumed between the values produced by **NOW** in different components of a parallel construct. Occam neither requires nor supports a global sense of time.

Care needs to be taken when regarding the time as an integer. Properly, **NOW** should be regarded as unsigned, in which case note that the time represented by all ones increments to zero. If regarded as a two's complement integer then the largest positive integer value is incremented to the most negative value. The **AFTER** operator gives the desired results, regardless of the sign of **NOW** or of the time it is being compared with.

See also

3.3.4	**Wait processes**
3.7.6	**Clock comparison operator**

3.8.4 Character constants

Character constants yield the ASCII representation of a character.

'a'	the ASCII for the character **a**
'*''	the ASCII for the quote character
'*n'	the ASCII for the newline character
'*#ff'	the ASCII for the erase character

The syntactic category char.const is informally defined as any occam character (except * and quote marks), or a special character sequence (defined below), placed between single quotes. It evaluates to the corresponding ASCII code, without parity.

Some codes (such as those of newline, quote marks and asterisk itself) are written as an asterisk followed by a character as follows

*c	*C	carriage return
*n	*N	newline
*t	*T	horizontal tabulate
*s	*S	space
*'		quotation mark
*"		double quotation mark
**		asterisk

Any other code is written as an asterisk, followed by a two digit hexadecimal constant (introduced by #).

Note that the character constant for single quote must be written as '*''.

See also

3.9.2   **Character set**

3.8.5 Vector constants (TABLE)

A table produces a vector of constants

```
DEF crctable   = TABLE [ #0000, #CC01, #D801, #1400,
                         #F001, #3C00, #2800, #E401,
                         #A001, #6C00, #7800, #B401,
                         #5000, #9C01, #8801, #4400
                       ] :
```

defines a vector constant. Individual values may be obtained by subscripting from the identifier **crctable**, and the identifier may be passed as a vector value parameter in the substitution of a named process.

table   = TABLE [[BYTE] expression {, expression}]

A table is a vector constant. It may be used anywhere that a vector identifier may be used, but may not be assigned to. Each member of the table must be a constant expression.

If the keyword **BYTE** is used, then each constant is truncated to byte size and a byte vector created.

See also

3.5.3	**Vectors of variables**
3.7	**Expressions and constant expressions**
3.8.6	**Character strings**

3.8.6 Character strings

A string produces a table of byte constants.

"Hello World*N"

a string of 12 characters, terminated by the newline character.

A string is written as a sequence of characters placed between double quote (") marks. Each character is written using the same conventions as for character constants. Within a string the double quote character must be written as *".

A string is represented as a table of byte constants. The first byte gives the number of characters in the string, the remaining bytes are set to the ASCII representations of the characters in the string. A string is limited to not more than 255 characters. The null string consists of a single byte set to zero.

A string may be written anywhere that a vector identifier may be used. It is not valid to assign to a string.

See also

3.5.3	Vectors of variables
3.8.4	Character constants
3.8.5	Vector constants

3.9 Lexical and character representations
3.9.1 Identifiers and reserved words

An identifier consists of a sequence of letters (a to z, A to Z), decimal digits (0 to 9) and dots (.), the first of which must be a letter. Uppercase and lowercase letters are not differentiated.

Certain identifiers are reserved as keywords to identify language constructs.

AFTER
ALLOCATE
ALT
AND
ANY
BYTE
CHAN
DEF
FALSE
FOR
IF
LOAD
NOT
NOW
OR
PAR
PLACED
PORT
PRI
PROC
SEQ
SKIP
TABLE
TRUE
VALUE
VAR
WAIT
WHILE

Other identifiers may also be associated in a given implementation with channels and named processes which provide interfaces with the runtime environment.

3.9.2 Character set

The occam character set comprises

Alphabetic characters

A B C D E F G H I J K L M N O P Q R S T U V W X Y Z
a b c d e f g h i j k l m n o p q r s t u v w x y z

Digits

0 1 2 3 4 5 6 7 8 9

Other characters

! " # % & ' ( ) * + , − . / : ; < = > ? @ [\ ]

The space character

Note that some terminals may not support lowercase letters.

Other characters from the ASCII character set may be used in strings and character constants where supported by the implementation.

3.10 Syntax
3.10.1 Program format

Occam uses indentation from the left hand margin to indicate program structure. The indentation is indicated informally for each construct in the main body of the manual, which also contains examples

Each process starts on a new line, at a level of indentation given by the following rules

Constructs

The construct keyword and an optional replicator occupy the first line. Each of the component processes (if any) start on a new line and are indented by two spaces more than the construct keyword.

Guarded processes

The expression and/or input or wait occupies the first line. The component process starts on the following line, indented two more spaces.

Conditional processes

The expression occupies the first line. The component process starts on the following line, indented two more spaces.

Declarations

Each declaration starts on a new line, at the same level of indentation as the process it prefixes. The final line of a declaration is terminated by a colon.

Blank lines may be inserted anywhere and are ignored.

A construct may be broken to occupy more than one line. Line breaks may occur after comma, semi-colon, before the second operand of an operator which takes two operands, and after the **&** of a guard. The continuation must be more indented than the first line of the construct. A string may be broken by terminating it with a double quote mark, and then starting its continuation on the next line (more indented than the first line of the construct) with a further double quote mark.

3.10.1 Program format
Continued

Spaces are required to define indentation, and to separate identifiers. Spaces may not occur within identifiers or operators. Otherwise, extra spaces may be freely used to improve readability.

Comments are introduced by double hyphen (--), and terminate at the end of the line. All the characters of a comment, including the double hyphen, are ignored. A comment may follow an occam construct on the same line, or may occupy a line by itself. For editing convenience, a comment occurring on a line by itself should be started at the same or greater level of indentation as the following construct.

3.10.2   Syntax summary

The following four syntactic categories are defined informally in the main part of the manual

identifier (3.9.1)
number (3.8.2)
char.const (3.8.4)
string (3.8.6)

Processes

```
program          = process
process          = primitive
                 | construct
                 | identifier [ ( expression { , expression} ) ]
                 | declaration : process
```

Primitive processes

```
assignment       = variable := expression
input            = channel ? variable { ; variable}
                 | channel ? ANY
output           = channel ! expression { ; expression}
                 | channel ! ANY
wait             = WAIT expression
primitive        = assignment|input|output|wait|SKIP
```

Constructors

```
guard            = [expression & ] input
                 | [expression & ] wait
                 | [expression & ] SKIP
guarded.process  = guard process
                 | ALT {guarded.process}
                 | ALT replicator guarded.process
conditional      = expression process
                 | IF {conditional}
                 | IF replicator conditional
replicator       = identifier = [ expression FOR expression]
construct        = SEQ {process}
                 | PAR {process}
                 | ALT {guarded.process}
                 | IF {conditional}
                 | SEQ replicator process
                 | PAR replicator process
                 | ALT replicator guarded.process
                 | IF replicator conditional
                 | WHILE expression process
```

3.10.2 Syntax summary
Continued

Declarations

subscript	=	[[BYTE] expression]
chan	=	identifier [[expression]]
var	=	identifier [subscript]
const.def	=	identifier = expression
	|	identifier = vector.constant
form.parm	=	VAR identifier [[]] {, identifier [[]]}
	|	CHAN identifier [[]] {, identifier [[]]}
	|	VALUE identifier [[]] {, identifier [[]]}
form.parms	=	(form.parm {, form.parm})
declaration	=	VAR var {, var}
	|	CHAN chan {, chan}
	|	DEF const.def {, const.def}
	|	PROC identifier [form.parms] = process

Expressions

variable	=	identifier [subscript]
channel	=	identifier [[expression]]
vector.constant	=	table l string
item	=	variable l vector.constant subscript
table	=	TABLE [[BYTE] expression {, expression}]
arithmetic.op	=	+ l − l * l / l \
comparison.op	=	< l > l <= l >= l = l <> l = l AFTER
logical.op	=	/\ l \/ l ><
boolean.op	=	AND l OR
shift.op	=	<< l >>
monadic.op	=	− l NOT
assoc.op	=	+ l * l logical.op l boolean.op
operator	=	arithmetic.op l comparison.op l logical.op
	|	boolean.op l shift.op
element	=	number l item l TRUE l FALSE l NOW
	|	char.const l (expression)
expression	=	element {assoc.op element}
	|	element [operator element]
	|	monadic.op element

3.10.2 Syntax summary
Continued

Vector operations

assignment	= destination := source
output	= channel ! slice
input	= channel ? slice
destination	= slice
source	= slice
slice	= identifier [[BYTE] base FOR count]
base	= expression
count	= expression

Configuration

program	= system
system	= PLACED PAR {system}
	| PLACED PAR replicator system
	| {declaration :} system
	| allocation : singleton
allocation	= ALLOCATE processor
	{ PORT port.allocation }
	[LOAD port]
	[other.allocations]
processor	= expression
port.allocation	= port :–channel [, channel]
port	= expression
singleton	= {declaration :} singleton
	| PRI PAR {process}
	| process
construct	= PRI ALT { guarded.process }
	| PRI ALT replicator guarded.process

3.11 Vector operations

Slices extend the primitive assignment, input and output processes to allow efficient assignment and communication of parts of vectors.

These facilities may be omitted in simple implementations.

3.11.1 Slices

A slice identifies part of a vector.

slice	=	identifier [[BYTE] base FOR count]
base	=	expression
count	=	expression

A slice identifies a set of vector elements. The elements may be words or bytes. The identifier must be declared as a vector of variables or a constant vector. The expression base is the subscript of the first element in the set, and the number of elements is given by count. A slice must have at least one element.

Slices may be used in assignment, input and output processes.

A slice of word elements may be used as an actual parameter in a substitution. A slice of a vector of variables may be substituted for a vector of variables or a vector of values. A slice of a constant vector may only be substituted for a vector of values.

3.11.2 Slice assignment

An assignment transfers the elements of a slice to another slice.

assignment = destination := source
destination = slice
source = slice

The source and destination slices must be of the same length, and must not overlap. Both must be word slices or both must be byte slices.

The value of each element of the destination slice is set to the value of the corresponding element of the source slice. The assignment then terminates.

The destination may not be a slice of a constant vector.

3.11.3 Slice communication

Slice communication transfers the values in a slice from an output process to an input process.

in.pack ? p.buff[BYTE n FOR 16]

inputs a **16** byte slice from **in.pack** and places the received data into the vector **p.buff** starting at byte number **n**.

output   = channel ! slice
input   = channel ? slice

Slice communication is similar to communication of a single value except that a number of values are copied in a single communication. Communication occurs when both an input process and an output process are ready, and the effect is to set the value of each element in the input slice to the value of the corresponding element of the output slice.

The input and output slices in any slice communication must be of equal length. Both must be word slices or both must be byte slices. The input slice may not be a slice of a constant vector.

A slice input may be used in the guard of a guarded process.

3.12 Configuration

Configuration associates the components of an occam program with a set of physical resources.

Configuration is used to meet speed and response requirements by distributing programs over separate, interconnected computers, and by placing and prioritising processes on single computers.

Every computer has local store and a set of numbered ports. A physical connection between two computers connects a port on one computer to a port on the other computer. This implements up to two channels between the computers, one in each direction.

A parallel construct may be configured for a network of computers. Each computer executes a component process, and port allocations are used to allocate channels to ports.

A parallel construct may be configured for an individual computer. The computer shares its time between the component processes, and the channels are implemented by values in store. Indeed, a parallel construct configured for a network may be reconfigured for an individual computer.

On any individual computer, a parallel construct may be configured to prioritise its components, and an alternative construct may be configured to prioritise its inputs.

The allocation of processing resources to the concurrent processes in a program does not affect the logical behaviour of the program. Simple implementations may omit or ignore some or all of the configuration facilities.

3.12.1 Prioritised alternative processes (PRI ALT)

Alternative processes may be prioritised.

```
VAR going :
SEQ
   going := TRUE
   WHILE going
      VAR x:
      PRI ALT
         stop ? ANY
            going := FALSE
         c1 ? x
         c2 ! x
```

                    c1 → [x] → c2
                          ↑
                         stop

This program copies values from channel **c1** to channel **c2**. Any input on channel **stop** stops the copying action. If both channels **c1** and **stop** are ready to input, **stop** is selected.

construct   =   PRI ALT
                    { guarded . process }
              | PRI ALT replicator
                    guarded . process

If more than one guarded process is ready when a prioritised alternative process is executed, the first one in textual sequence is selected.

If more than one guarded process becomes ready at the same time, an arbitrary one is selected. This may occur if they contain inputs on the same channel.

See also

3.4.3   **Alternative processes**

3.12.2 Single processor execution and priority (PRI PAR)

A singleton is a process executed by a single processor.

CHAN edit.in, edit.out:
PRI PAR
   terminal.io (keyboard, screen, edit.in, edit.out)
   editor (edit.in, edit.out)

always executes the terminal input and output in preference to the editor.

singleton   = {declaration :}
                 singleton
           | PRI PAR
                 { process}
           | process

A singleton is a set of declarations and processes to be executed by a single processor.

A prioritised parallel contruct gives each component process a different priority. The first component has the highest priority and the last component has the lowest priority. An implementation may restrict the number of components which a prioritised parallel construct can have.

A prioritised parallel construct ensures that a higher priority process always proceeds in preference to a lower priority one. The progress of a higher priority process is not affected by any lower priority one, except by communication on connecting channels. If several concurrent processes at the same priority are able to proceed, each one is given an opportunity to proceed in turn.

3.12.3 Multi-processor execution (PLACED PAR)

A system is a parallel construct which is configured for a network of computers. Each computer with local store executes a component process.

system = PLACED PAR
     {system}
   | PLACED PAR replicator
    system
   | {declaration :}
    system
   | allocation :
    singleton

The configuration of a system is described by a set of declarations and parallel constructs. The declarations may not include declarations of variables or vectors of variables.

Each computer executes a component singleton of the placed parallel construct. Each channel between such singletons must be associated with a port on each of the corresponding computers, and the two ports must be physically connected together.

See also

3.12.4 **Physical resource allocation**

3.12.4 Physical resource allocation (ALLOCATE)

Allocations are used to give physical resources to processes and channels.

```
CHAN comms:
PLACED PAR
  ALLOCATE 0
    PORT 0:- comms
    PORT 1:- c1
    LOAD 1:
  buffer (c1, comms)
  ALLOCATE 1
    PORT 0:- comms
    PORT 1:- c2
    LOAD 0:
  buffer (comms, c2)
```

c1 → □ — comms → □ → c2

places a buffer process on each of two processors. Ports are allocated for the channels and for loading the programs to be executed by each processor.

```
allocation    = ALLOCATE processor
                  {PORT port.allocation}
                  [LOAD port]
                  [other.allocations]

processor      = expression
port.allocation = port:- channel [, channel]
port           = expression
```

Each singleton in a system is given resources by an allocation.

The physical processors in a system are identified and distinguished by giving each one a unique number. The processor number is the value of the expression at the start of the allocation.

Every processor has a set of numbered ports. A physical connection between two processors connects a port on one processor to a port on the other processor. This implements up to two channels between the processors, one in each direction.

A port is associated with one or two of the channels used in the singleton. If there are two channels, the singleton must use one channel for input, the other channel for output. The channel used in a port allocation may be a simple channel, or an element of a vector of channels.

3.12.4 Physical resource allocation (ALLOCATE)
Continued

A channel may occur in only one port allocation within an allocation.

The **LOAD** allocation nominates a port from which a process will be loaded when the system is initialised. Loading takes place from a single point, and the load ports must be allocated so as to provide a route from this point to each processor in the system. The load route must exist as physical connections between the processors in the system, but need not correspond to the connections indicated by the port allocations.

Some implementations may require further information to complete the allocation of resources, for example the address from which code should be loaded. A description of these allocations is found in the appropriate implementation reference manual.

See also

3.12.3   **Multi-processor execution**

Index

4   Index
Continued

:=	2.1	**3.3.1**	3.10.2	**3.11.2**						
?	2.1	**3.3.2**	3.10.2	**3.11.3**						
!	2.1	**3.3.3**	3.10.2	**3.11.3**						
;	**3.3.2**	**3.3.3**	3.10.2							
:	2.2	**3.5**	3.5.1	3.5.2	3.5.3	3.5.4	3.5.5	3.6	3.10.1	
	3.10.2									
&	2.7	**3.4.3**	3.10.2							
=	2.8	**3.4.6**	3.5.5	**3.6**	3.7.2	3.10.2	**3.12.4**			
,	3.5.1	3.5.2	3.5.3	3.5.4	3.5.5	**3.6**	**3.8.5**	3.10.1	3.10.2	
+	**3.7.1**	3.10.2								
-	**3.7.1**	3.10.2								
'	**3.8.4**									
"	**3.8.4**	3.8.6								
--	**3.10.1**									
*	**3.7.1**	3.8.4	3.10.2							
/	**3.7.1**	3.10.2								
\	**3.7.1**	3.10.2								
<	**3.7.2**	3.10.2								
>	**3.7.2**	3.10.2								
<=	**3.7.2**	3.10.2								
>=	**3.7.2**	3.10.2								
<>	**3.7.2**	3.10.2								
/\	**3.7.3**	3.10.2								
\/	**3.7.3**	3.10.2								
><	**3.7.3**	3.10.2								
>>	**3.7.5**	3.10.2								
<<	**3.7.5**	3.10.2								
*C	**3.8.4**									
*N	**3.8.4**									
*T	**3.8.4**									
*S	**3.8.4**									
*'	**3.8.4**									
*"	**3.8.4**									
**	**3.8.4**									
#	**3.8.2**	3.8.4								
[]	2.8	**3.4.6**	**3.5.3**	**3.5.4**	**3.6**	3.8.1	**3.8.5**	3.10.2	**3.11.1**	
	3.11.3									
()	2.6	**3.6**	**3.8.1**	3.10.2						

Index
Continued

actual parameters	2.5	**3.6**						
AFTER	3.3.4	**3.7.6**	3.8.3	3.9.1	3.10.2			
ALLOCATE	3.10.2	**3.12.4**						
allocation	3.10.2	3.12.3	**3.12.4**					
allocation, store	**3.5**							
ALT	2.7	3.3.2	3.3.3	3.3.4	**3.4.3**	3.4.6	3.9.1	3.10.2 **3.12.1**
alternative processes	2.7	3.2	3.3.2	3.3.4	**3.4.3**	**3.12.1**		
and	**3.7.3**							
AND	3.7	**3.7.4**	3.9.1	3.10.2				
ANY	2.7	2.8	**3.3.2**	**3.3.3**	3.9.1	3.10.2		
arithmetic	**3.7.1**	3.10.2						
arrays of channels	2.8	3.4.6	**3.5.4**					
of processes	2.8	**3.4.6**						
of variables	3.4.6	**3.5.3**	**3.11**					
ASCII	3.8.1	3.8.4	3.8.6	**3.9.2**				
assignment processes	2.1	**3.3.1**	3.4.2	3.4.6	3.5	3.5.1	3.6	3.10.2 **3.11.2**
associative operators	**3.7**	3.10.2						
asterisk	**3.7.1**	**3.8.4**	3.10.2					
Backus-Naur form	**3.2**							
base	**3.4.6**	3.8.1	**3.11.1**					
bit manipulation	**3.7.2**	**3.7.3**	**3.7.5**	3.8.1	3.8.2			
Boolean operators	3.7	**3.7.4**	3.10.2					
brackets	3.2	3.6	**3.8.1**					
curly	**3.2**							
round	2.6	**3.6**	**3.8.1**	3.10.2				
square	2.8	3.2	**3.4.6**	**3.5.3**	**3.5.4**	**3.6**	3.8.1	**3.8.5** 3.10.2
BYTE	3.3.1	3.3.2	3.3.3	3.4.6	3.5.3	3.5.5	3.6	**3.8.1** 3.8.5
	3.8.6	3.9.1	3.10.2	3.11.1				
carriage return	**3.8.4**							
CHAN	2.4	2.6	2.8	3.3.2	3.3.3	3.4.2	3.4.6	3.5 **3.5.2**
	3.5.4	3.6	3.9.1	3.10.2				
channel declarations	2.4	2.6	2.8	**3.5.2**	3.5.4			
channels	1	2.1	2.4	2.5	2.6	2.8	3.3.2	3.3.3 3.4.2
	3.4.3	3.4.6	3.5	**3.5.2**	3.5.4	3.6	3.8.1	3.9.1 3.12
	3.12.3	3.12.4						
character codes	**3.8.4**							
character constants	3.5.5	3.7	3.8.1	**3.8.4**	3.8.5	3.8.6	3.9	3.9.2
character set	**3.9.2**							
character strings	3.5.5	**3.8.6**						

Index
Continued

clock	3.3.4	3.7.6	**3.8.3**					
clock comparison operator	**3.7.6**							
colon	2.2	**3.5**	3.10.1					
comma	**3.10.1**							
comments	**3.10.1**							
communication	1	2.1	2.4	2.5	3.3.2	3.3.3	**3.4.2**	3.11	3.11.3
	3.12.2							
comparison operators	**3.7.2**	3.10.2						
component processes	3.3.2	3.3.3	**3.4**	3.4.1	3.4.2	3.4.3	3.4.4	3.4.5	3.4.6
	3.5	3.6	3.8.3	3.10.1	3.12.1	3.12.2		
concurrent processes	1	2.1	2.4	2.5	2.8	3.3.2	3.3.3	**3.4.2**	3.4.6
	3.5.2	3.5.4	3.12	**3.12.2**	**3.12.3**			
conditional processes	**3.4.4**	3.10.1	3.10.2					
configuration	**3.12**							
constants	2.7	3.4.6	3.5	3.5.3	3.5.4	**3.5.5**	3.6	3.7	3.7.3
	3.7.5	3.8.1	3.8.2	3.8.4	3.8.5	3.8.6	3.9.2	3.10.2	
character	**3.8.4**							
vector	**3.8.5**							
constant definitions	2.7	**3.5.5**						
constant expressions	3.5.5	**3.7**						
constructs	2.2	3.2	**3.4**	3.6	3.9.1	3.10.1	3.10.2		
alternative	2.7	**3.4.3**	3.12.1					
conditional	**3.4.4**							
parallel	2.4	**3.4.2**	**3.12.2**	**3.12.3**				
repetitive	2.3	**3.4.5**						
replicators	2.8	**3.4.6**						
sequential	2.2	**3.4.1**						
constructors	2.2	3.4.6	**3.10.1**					
continuation lines	**3.10.1**							
count	**3.4.6**	**3.11.1**						
curly brackets	**3.2**							
decimals	**3.8.2**	3.9.1						
declarations	**3.5**	3.10.1	3.10.2	3.12.2	3.12.3			
channels	2.4	**3.5.2**						
constant definitions	2.7	**3.5.5**						
formal parameters	2.6	**3.6**						
named processes	2.6	**3.6**						
replicator indices	2.8	**3.4.6**						
variables	2.2	**3.5.1**						

4 Index
Continued

declarations vectors of channels	2.8	**3.5.4**						
vectors of variables	**3.5.3**							
DEF	2.7	3.3.4	3.4.6	3.5	**3.5.5**	3.7.6	3.8.5	3.9.1	3.10.2
definitions	2.7	**3.5.5**						
delays	3.3.2	3.3.3	**3.3.4**					
destination	3.10.2	**3.11.2**						
digits	3.8.2	**3.9.1**						
division	**3.7.1**							
dots	**3.9.1**							
down shift	**3.7.5**							
double hyphen	**3.10.1**							
elements	3.7	**3.8**	3.8.1	3.10.2				
elements of vectors	3.3.1	3.3.2	3.3.3	3.5.3	3.5.4	3.6	**3.8.1**	3.11.1
equals	**3.4.6**	**3.7.2**						
erase	**3.8.4**							
escape	**3.8.4**	3.8.6						
exclusive or	**3.7.3**							
expressions	2.1	2.7	3.2	3.3.1	3.3.3	3.3.4	3.4.2	3.4.3	3.4.4
	3.4.5	3.4.6	3.5	3.5.3	3.5.4	3.5.5	3.6	**3.7**	3.7.6
	3.8.1	3.8.5	3.10.1	3.10.2				
FALSE	2.3	3.4.5	3.5.5	3.7	3.7.2	3.7.4	**3.8.1**	3.9.1	3.10.2
FOR	2.8	**3.4.6**	3.9.1	3.10.2	**3.11.1**			
formal parameters	2.6	3.5	**3.6**					
format	**3.10.1**							
free variables	**3.6**							
greater than operator	**3.7.2**	3.10.1						
guard	2.7	3.3.2	3.3.4	**3.4.3**	3.10.1	3.10.2		
guarded processes	2.7	**3.4.3**	3.4.6	3.10.1	3.10.2	3.12.1		
hexadecimal constant	3.7.3	**3.8.2**	3.8.4					
identifiers	3.4.6	3.5	3.6	3.8.1	**3.9.1**			
IF	**3.4.4**	3.9.1	3.10.2					
indentation	2.2	2.6	3.4.1	3.4.2	3.4.5	3.5	**3.10.1**		
input processes	1	2.1	2.5	2.8	**3.3.2**	3.3.3	3.4.2	3.4.3	3.4.6
	3.5	3.10.1	3.10.2	**3.11.3**				
integers	3.7.1	3.7.2	**3.8.2**					
item	**3.8.1**	3.10.2						
keywords	2.2	3.2	**3.10.1**					
left shift	**3.7.5**							
less than operator	**3.7.2**	3.10.1						

Index
Continued

lexical representations	**3.9**							
line breaks	**3.10.1**							
LOAD	**3.10.2**	3.12.4						
local clock	1	3.3.4	3.7.6	**3.8.3**				
locations of store	1	**3.5**						
logical operators	**3.7.3**	3.10.2						
loop	2.3	2.8	**3.4.5**	**3.4.6**				
lowercase	**3.9.1**							
masking	**3.7.3**							
minus operator	**3.7.1**							
monadic operators	**3.7**	3.10.2						
multiplication	**3.7.1**							
named processes	2.6	3.5	**3.6**	3.8.5	3.12.3			
newline	3.4.2	**3.8.4**	3.8.6	3.10.1				
Newton-Raphson	**2.8**							
NOT	3.7	**3.7.3**	3.9.1	3.10.2				
NOW	3.3.4	3.7.6	3.8.1	**3.8.3**	3.9.1	3.10.2		
null string	**3.8.6**							
null message	**3.3.2**	3.3.3						
numbers	3.5.5	3.7	3.8.1	**3.8.2**	3.10.2			
operators	3.5.5	**3.7**						
arithmetic	**3.7.1**							
Boolean	**3.7.4**							
clock comparison	**3.7.6**							
comparison	**3.7.2**							
logical	**3.7.3**							
shift	**3.7.5**							
or	**3.7.3**							
OR	3.7	**3.7.4**	3.9.1	3.10.2				
output processes	1	2.1	2.5	2.8	3.3.2	**3.3.3**	3.4.2	3.4.3	3.10.2
	3.11.3							
PAR	2.4	2.8	3.3.2	3.3.3	**3.4.2**	3.4.6	3.5.1	3.5.2	3.5.4
	3.9.1	3.10.2	3.12.2	3.12.3	3.12.4			
parallel processes	1	2.1	2.4	2.5	2.8	3.3.2	3.3.3	**3.4.2**	3.4.6
	3.5.2	3.5.4	3.12	**3.12.2**	**3.12.3**			
parameters	2.6	3.5	3.5.3	3.5.4	3.5.5	**3.6**	3.8.5		
parentheses	**3.8.1**							
pipeline	2.8							
PLACED PAR	3.10.2	**3.12.3**	3.12.4					

4 Index
Continued

plus operator		**3.7.1**						
PORT		3.10.2	**3.12.4**					
precedence		**3.8.1**						
prefixed process		2.6	**3.6**	3.10.1				
PRI ALT		3.10.2	**3.12.1**					
primitive processes		**3.3**	3.3.1	3.3.2	3.3.3	3.3.4	3.10.2	
PRI PAR		3.10.2	**3.12.2**					
priority		3.12	3.12.1	**3.12.2**				
PROC		2.6	3.5	**3.6**	3.9.1	3.10.2		
processes	alternative	2.7	**3.4.3**	**3.12.1**				
	assignment	2.1	**3.3.1**	**3.11.2**				
	component	**3.4**						
	concurrent	2.4	**3.4.2**	3.12.2	3.12.3			
	conditional	**3.4.4**						
	guarded	2.7	**3.4.3**					
	input	2.1	**3.3.2**	**3.11.3**				
	named	2.6	**3.6**					
	output	2.1	**3.3.3**	**3.11.3**				
	parallel	2.4	**3.4.2**	3.12.2	3.12.3			
	prefixed	2.6	**3.6**					
	primitive	2.1	**3.3**					
	repetitive	2.3	**3.4.5**					
	sequential	2.2	**3.4.1**					
	skip	**3.3.5**						
	wait	**3.3.4**						
processor allocation		**3.12.4**						
ready		1	2.7	**3.3.3**	**3.3.4**	3.4.2	3.4.3	3.4.6
recursion		**3.6**						
remainder operator		**3.7.1**						
repetitive processes		2.3	**3.4.5**					
replicators		2.8	**3.4.6**					
right shift		**3.7.5**						
round brackets		2.6	**3.6**	**3.8.1**	3.10.2			
scope		**3.5**						
SEQ		2.2	2.3	2.8	**3.4.1**	3.4.3	3.4.5	3.4.6	3.5.1	3.9.1
		3.10.2						
sequential processes		2.2	**3.4.1**					
shift operators		**3.7.5**	3.10.2					
singleton		3.10.2	**3.12.3**	3.12.4				

Index
Continued

SKIP	**3.3.5**	3.4.3	3.10.2					
slices	3.11	**3.11.1**	3.11.2	3.11.3				
source	3.10.2	**3.11.2**						
spaces	3.8.4	3.9.2	**3.10.1**					
square brackets	2.8	3.2	**3.4.6**	**3.5.3**	**3.5.4**	**3.6**	3.8.1	**3.8.5**	3.10.2
store	1	**3.5**						
strings	3.5.5	3.8.1	3.8.5	**3.8.6**	3.9.2	3.10.1		
subscription	2.8	3.3.1	3.3.2	3.4.2	3.5.3	3.5.4	3.5.5	**3.8.1**	3.10.2
substitution	2.6	3.5.3	3.5.4	3.5.5	**3.6**	3.8.5		
subtraction operator	**3.7.1**							
synchronisation	1	2.5	**3.3.2**	**3.3.3**	**3.4.3**			
syntax	**3.2**	3.10	3.10.2					
syntax summary	**3.10.2**							
system	3.10.2	**3.12.3**						
tab character	**3.7.4**							
TABLE	3.5.5	3.7.3	3.7.4	3.8.1	**3.8.5**	3.8.6	3.9.1	3.10.2
time	3.3.4	3.7.6	**3.8.3**					
timeout	**3.3.4**							
TRUE	2.3	2.4	2.6	2.7	2.8	3.3.4	3.4.2	3.4.3	3.4.4
	3.4.5	3.4.6	3.5.5	3.6	3.7	3.7.1	3.7.2	3.7.4	3.7.6
	3.8.1	3.9.1	3.10.2					
up shift	**3.7.5**							
uppercase	**3.9.1**							
VALUE	**3.6**	3.9.1	3.10.2					
VAR	2.2	2.3	2.4	2.6	2.7	2.8	3.3.4	3.4.1	3.4.2
	3.4.3	3.4.5	3.4.6	3.5	**3.5.1**	3.5.3	3.6	**3.7.6**	3.9.1
	3.10.2							
variable declarations	2.2	**3.5.1**	3.5.3	3.6	3.10.2			
vector constants	**3.8.5**							
vectors	**3.5**	3.5.3	3.5.4	3.6	3.8.1	3.8.5	3.8.6	3.11
vectors of channels	2.8	**3.5.4**	3.12.3					
vectors of variables	**3.5.3**							
vector operations	**3.11**							
WAIT	**3.3.4**	3.4.3	3.7.6	3.8.3	3.9.1	3.10.2		
WHILE	2.3	2.4	2.6	2.7	2.8	**3.4.5**	3.9.1	3.10.2
word	3.3.1	3.3.2	3.7.1	3.7.5	3.7.6	**3.8.1**	3.8.3	